From This Day Forward

By
Patricia A Fisher

**Published by
ITSMEEE™ Industries
Aurora CO 80012
USA**

Patricia A Fisher

From This Day Forward

Patricia A Fisher

Other Titles By
Patricia A. Fisher

With Love ITSMEEE™
Copyright ©1997 by Patricia A
Fisher

With Love ITSMEEE™ II
Copyright © 1998 by Patricia A.
Fisher

*Introducing Number III
ITSMEEE™*
ITSMEEE™ Industries
Copyright © 1999 by Patricia A.
Fisher

*ITSMEEE™ On My Journey
Home*
Copyright © 1999 by Patricia A.
Fisher
ITSMEEE™ Industries

Other Titles By
Patricia A. Fisher

Hello, ITSMEEE™ Again
Copyright © 2002 by Patricia A.
Fisher
ITSMEEE™ Industries

ITSMEEE™ Beneath The Grey
An Autobiography
Copyright ©2003 by Patricia A.
Fisher
ITSMEEE™ Industries

From This Day Forward
Copyright © 2003 by Patricia A.
Fisher
ITSMEEE™ Industries

I Want to LIVE!
Copyright © 1999 by Patricia A.
Fisher
ITSMEEE™ Industries

Other Titles By
Patricia A. Fisher

Walk a Mile in Our Shoes
Copyright © 2005 by Patricia A.
Fisher
ITSMEEE™ Industries

.

The Favor I Owe the World
Copyright © 2005 by Patricia A.
Fisher
ITSMEEE™ Industries

Home Is Where We Park It!
Copyright © 2008 by Pat Fisher
Funhous Publishing

The Absence of Awful
Copyright © 2012 by Patricia A.
Fisher
ITSMEEE™ Industries

Table of contents:

Dear Gentle Reader,

I would like to believe that marriage is still in style and divorce is dwindling.

I would like to believe that our favorite clothes will last, year After year and still fit when we put them on...

I would like to believe that we cherish the elderly. I've seen the sparkle in their eyes. They know things about life and they are wise. Their bodies are old, **but their minds are young.**

I want people to know that adults are just as important as children. Let us not ignore them because they are aging.

Speaking with my Mom would be grand! She is here in spirit, but not in the flesh...

Wouldn't it be neat, if we could
all live in peace, and enjoy good
health while on our journeys?

The world keeps flourishing, as
life longs for itself... I give thanks
for my part in this plan.

When I was a child, I had this
idea that we humans were not
plugged into an electrical outlet.
I could not understand how we
were still moving around! That
wonder of life still intrigues me...

There are so many people, living
a life of service, who are not as
obvious as doctors and nurses.
They are people who wash pans,
or they are actors and actresses.
They are candle stick makers,
seamstresses, bus drivers, and
insurance salespersons... The
world is full of gentle souls, who
stand up tall and say, "I make a
difference!"

I will say again, "We are all in the same boat". Remember those tables at the carnivals? You take a hammer, and strike at manmade gophers. Each time one is pounded another one pops up somewhere else. This makes me think of the way humans affect each other – a chain reaction affect.

So may we hold love in high regard, and may we start a chain reaction of honoring each other.

Maybe we can start at home. Maybe we can excuse ourselves, and our families. For when we do, a whole new world opens up inside of us! We can then say, "We are just limited human beings – perfectly imperfect – and we forgive ourselves for this mistake".

The next time we go out into the
world we see that we really are
in the same boat.

We chuckle because we experience ourselves as being equal, and yet we are making a difference. We now find our uniqueness.

We begin to feel more connected and more secure.

Marriage can last longer, and be cherished. We renew our promise to God, and forever becomes a possibility.

Our elderly sense being less cut off, from the rest of the world, because all of us are feeling our value.

Maybe our magnificence will fill our minds, as we are really not plugged in!

May we feel that oneness with each other, build respect that has been sorely earned, and find humor.

We chuckle from learning this very, special secret-that we are indeed equal and yet unique, and that the universe needs every one of us.

It will be as if you are sitting on your own shoulder and witnessing the play that you are in. How incredibly fun it can be! For I have been doing most of these things!

Thank You
For Being a
Part of My
Journey!!
Patricia A. Fisher

Patricia A Fisher

Overwhelmed By
ITSMEEE™ Industries

I have been overwhelmed by the business end of writing and publishing my books. This has cut me off from what I started to do.

Watching a movie, starring Adam Sandler, reminded me of my beginnings. For he was kind to most people (not the ones that tried to treat him badly).

My company, ITSMEEE™ Industries, began with my thousands of phone calls to my Mom--who has now passed on. I would call her and sort of sing, "Hi Mom, ITSMEEE"! That's why there is so many E's in ITSMEEE.

When the fun of ITSMEEE Industries was no longer in sight, I saw my endeavor, and adventure, become drudgery and almost a curse...

Then I remembered what my original mission was. It was to be an instrument of love, truth, and respect, for myself and my fellow Earthlings. If I can share the love, the rest will come along by itself. For I believe that love is all encompassing.

I will now balance the fun and effort of sharing these things. May God help me find the scales in my heart for this purpose...

Affectionately,
Patricia A. Fisher

There are only two
Kinds of people in the
World:

Survivors
And
Nonsurvivors.

The Nonsurvivors
Are dead...

By
Dennis H. Fisher

Patricia A Fisher

My

   Husband

     Is

       A

        Precarious

Aquarius

Patricia A Fisher

A Tribute to 'My' Dennis

He is an unusual challenge...
He lights up my life with his
love... His memory is unlimited!
There is little he forgets...

When he hears, he really
'listens'. When he makes a
promise, he follows through. He
is a man of his word...

He is very practical. Yet, he can
really make me laugh - usually
by mirroring my own words back
to me!

He made a promise to God and
me, that he would stay married
for eternity. We have been
married almost 30 years, and he
is still devoted to our union...

He never preaches, but I know
by his actions that he is a man
of God...

Dennis is a Dionysian.
Dionysus is a Greek God of wine,
an ecstatic, orgiastic, or
irrational character...

Though he rarely drinks,
Dennis is a lover of fine wines,
and a bit orgiastic at times.
Ecstatic? "No". Irrational? "No".

But he likes wine,
and he is sort of sexy.
He always did look like a Greek
God in his boxer shorts...

'MY' GREEK GOD!

He is so kind, although he has
learned some bad habits from
me. He yells, but only after I do.
He argues, but only when I raise
my voice at him.

I don't know if he will ever
understand my rage and anger.
For he was raised in a family
that had to hold these feelings
back, or his Father would say,
"Go ahead and fight, but I get
the winner"!

This was the way he was raised,
and it was a double edge sword...
It caused Dennis to hold in his
anger, so much, that I think it
causes his breathing problem to
get worse.

Plus, fighting with me, is futile...
I win most of the time! After
many years, he 'found his
mouth'... I am glad for this,
because it might help his health.

His peaceful ways have him so
laid back, that he could stand up
and talk to the devil himself! If
they joined in an altercation,
Dennis would be so calm, the
devil would lose the fight!
I am told that the one who
raises his or her voice first,
usually loses in most arguments
here on Earth.

'My' Dennis went to college a
couple of years before we met.
He joined the Air Force for 4
years. He took some classes
through US WEST.

He wanted to become an engineer for the company. This was his occupation 'till he retired about 16 years later. He is now retired... and... I started a company... He doesn't even want to work for me...

Because of his upbringing, Dennis is still quite 'innocent'-- sort of like he was not raised on Earth. He knows just what to say, as if he actually studied people's minds and hearts. But he is not sneaky. He just knows...

Little girls flirt with him like crazy! Kids and animals love him... I guess I could include most people...

13

My Mom thought he had Jesus
eyes. She never trusted anyone-
- especially men-- but she trusted
Dennis with her very life!
And she loved him...

I will state, here, that they loved
and respected each other very
much. I never saw anything like
it!

We have since lost Mom.
It was very hard on us both,
but Dennis and I are managing
better now.

If there's anything I know about
this world, it is that there is
always change. When change
stops, there will be something
outrageously wrong. Nothing
will be alive or vital.
It would be the end of all life.

Well, Dennis worked for 27 years, and has no wish to go back to work. He was offered a promotion, at retirement, but he declined with a smile…

Dennis and I travel in our RV, now. We really are retired! Any business I must take care of can be done on the road.
See you there!

Pondering Sex And Lovemaking

What is the difference between sex and lovemaking?

The dictionary defines sex,
as the sexual urge, or instinct,
that manifests itself in behavior.
(sexual intercourse)

The dictionary explains that
lovemaking is the act of courting
or wooing.

Another dictionary says that
love is an intense, affectionate
concern for another person.

I did not read a single word that told me there was heart felt love in the act of only sex...

Love, on the other hand, speaks of affection displayed toward another person.

This is a hard piece to write. For I do not know what to share, and what not to. This is such a private issue...

Loving, to me, is when you just glow deep down inside, when your loved one looks at you a certain way. You just want to get closer. Hence, lovemaking...

The feelings of desire are so much stronger, when you really love somebody.

You want to become 'one' with
this person. You want to show
how much you love them in
every way you can think of.

If you can't think of the right
'moves', just wait 'till you love
someone.

The 'moves' happen
automatically, while you explore
new ways to celebrate your
significant other.

Yet, it appears that there are
complications. There are two
sets of feelings. There are two
sets of needs and wants. There
are two complex people!

One person may be enamored,
and the other may have issues
that have not been addressed.

Maybe one person has a different libido than the other-- wanting to make love less often, or more often, than you.

Mom use to say to me, "A good 'provider' is no good in bed, but at least he stays out of the bars!" She, also, use to talk about how so-and-so 'worshiped' so-and-so! I use to go nuts!

I hated it, also, when she said someone must have scrubbed himself with Ajax! She, also would say, "She is so ugly she's cute!" (I say, "Rest in peace Mom"!)

But, a man or woman provider, sometimes is so occupied with getting food, clothes and shelter, that they are on a different wave length. They're tired, preoccupied, and wanting peace and quiet... Yet, they are showing love in the best way they know how.

Also, one partner may have had a bad experience in the past. They may have been abused, and need an obscene amount of time to heal and trust! Maybe one of them is self conscious about their body, and they have low self-esteem. It could be they are insecure with the whole idea of showing physical love.

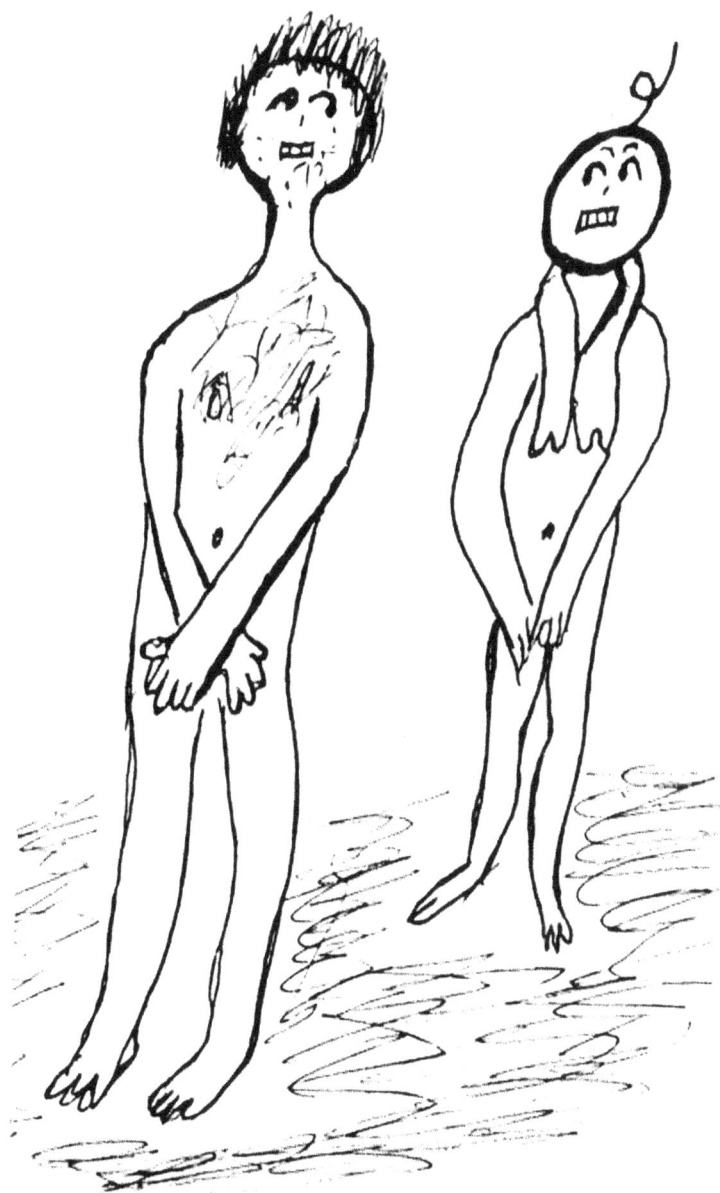

And, there are those who cannot seem to give up control in any situation. How would they trust someone, especially, if they were expected to be in the nude?

The world tells me that there is a balance. It's up to us to find it. Maybe, find some more interests. Or try something new to make your partner happy. You'll know what it is.

I believe that people, who only want sexual urges satisfied, are overwhelmed by the complications of being involved.

I've heard that some men can't
show their wives the same
desire, and physical attention,
that they can a mistress. It's
ironic that at the same time,
most of them love their wives!

Poets try to explain, in flowery
words, how love works.

There are tons of poems that
warm the hearts of lovers. Poets
try and try. Words just don't get
it--not completely--not in
matters of the heart.

But I urge you to give your heart
to someone, and hold someone
close. For even when I am not
trusting, I get back to knowing
that I love someone, and
someone truly loves me back.

And, when you just cannot understand the complexity of lovemaking and sex, try humor, two naked people, together, can most assuredly find something wonderfully funny to laugh at!

May God bless us all. And thank you for exploring this delicate subject with me.

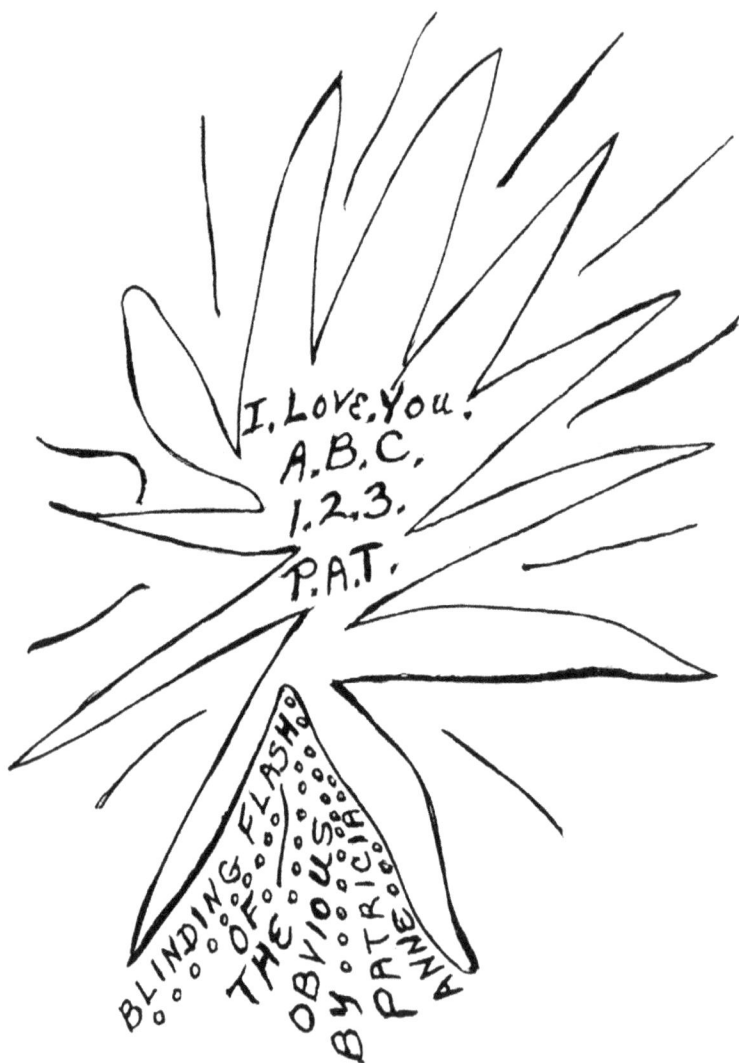

I. LOVE. YOU!
A.B.C.
1.2.3.
P.A.T.

BLINDING FLASH
OF
THE
OBVIOUS
BY
PATRICIA
ANNE

A Blinding Flash
of the Obvious

I'd always heard very sad stories about families breaking up because of mental illness. I use to feel fortunate that it was never going to happen to me...

Today I had a blinding flash of the obvious! My family's separateness is indeed caused by mental illness.

I don't know how many years I tried to bring our very broken family together. I would constantly fail, because it seemed like everyone fought this idea like the plague!

I just thought we were so dysfunctional that it might take awhile. So I waited. The years passed, and I just tried to be as loving as I could--not quite knowing the truth.

As I've told you, gentle reader, I would go home from family gatherings, and think that I had done something 'wrong'. I would get angry at myself for failing. The anger toward family would also be turned inward. These things would often make me get suicidal. Lots of times I would cry all the way home.

I would grill myself with questions like, "What will bring us together?" "What could I have done differently?" "What have I done that my family does not want to come over for the holidays?"

Recently, I have been counseled that my family may be afraid of doing something 'wrong' around me. They may fear making things worse. They may be afraid of another suicide in the family.

Maybe, they fear getting my disease, or, maybe they already have it.

It breaks my heart, when we stay so distant. Some family members openly want, or need, to just stay away...

The bigger picture is that my whole family has been effected by mental illness! Some of us actually have a mental illness. Some are sons and daughters, brothers and sisters, or husbands and wives of those who are afflicted.

I just realized today, that I can no longer take personally, the separateness of my family. No wonder I couldn't bring us together!

When we are around each other, we are like Mexican Jumping Beans. Early in life, we got very sensitized, by living closely with ill family members. This is partly why we are now reacting to each other.

It appears that we take things personally, when the fault lies within this terrible disease!

I love my family... I love them even more now that I am aware of these things.

We are all in the same boat-- hurting because of the suicides and attempted suicides. We may each feel the pain of being all alone-- not knowing that all of us are crying the same tears...

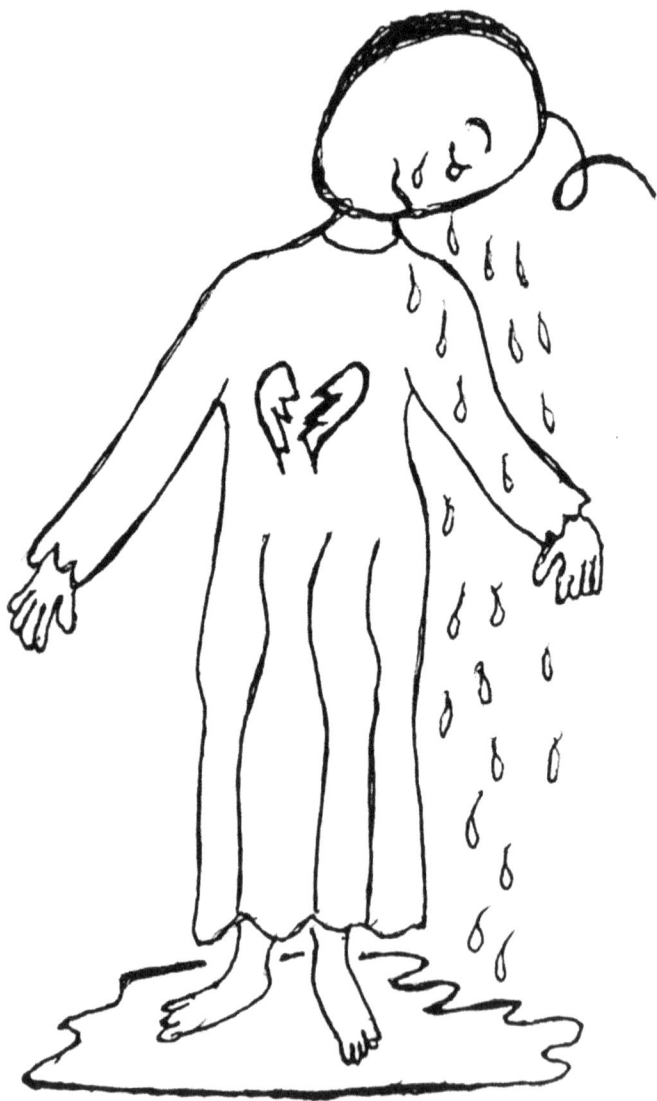

I have also lost friendships. One person was from way back in high school. The other relationship began about ten years later.

Even if they want to get back together, I don't want to subject myself to that kind of pain again. I must not have seen the writing on their wall that said, "Pat is not valid, because of her particular difficulty".

It saddens me when people see my illness first, and ignore the rest of me. I am not mentally ill. I have a mental illness. It only occupies part of me.

The other parts are of a person who can be funny, intelligent, sad, caring and lovable.

37

I have a mental illness. This does not mean I am weaker than others. I am strong everyday of my life. I have to be...

If asked, "What do I thrive on from others?" I would say, "I am most happy when people talk to me from a place of honesty, respect and caring."

I have been given these things, by mental health experts, for almost 35 years. They have trusted my validity, when I couldn't seem to trust it myself. They have shared huge amounts of their time with me, and, again, I am infinitely grateful.

I am loved by a good man. He has given me his constant support, and the kind of love I never knew about before him... For this, I am also grateful...

As for my family, I guess I'll never give up hope that a healing will take place. I pray that a sort of peace will be bestowed upon us, and make us free to love each other...

Nakiah Rain Weatherill,

I, your aunt, would like to welcome you into the world.

I would like, very much, to see you grow up. You are 8 months old, and I've never seen you. I love you anyway, and I bet you are beautiful!

I don't have all the answers, but I think love is the main answer.

Plus God wants you here or you would not be here.

Remember that we Earthlings are all equal. We are also a bit different from each other, and it appears the Earth has limitations.

If you get 80% or 90% of what you want, you can have a pretty good life.

I ask you to appreciate things like nature, smiles, compassion and good people.

The people who say mean things usually just need extra love. Yet, try not to stay around people who are a vexation to your spirit.

Every person in the world has a story to tell. It is a joy to hear them, if you can trust...

It appears that all humans struggle, but when we all hold onto each other, life is worthwhile.

I love you, Nakiah.

And, please don't forget to have fun.

Love,
Aunt Pat

NAKIAH RAIN
WEATHERILL
04-27-2002

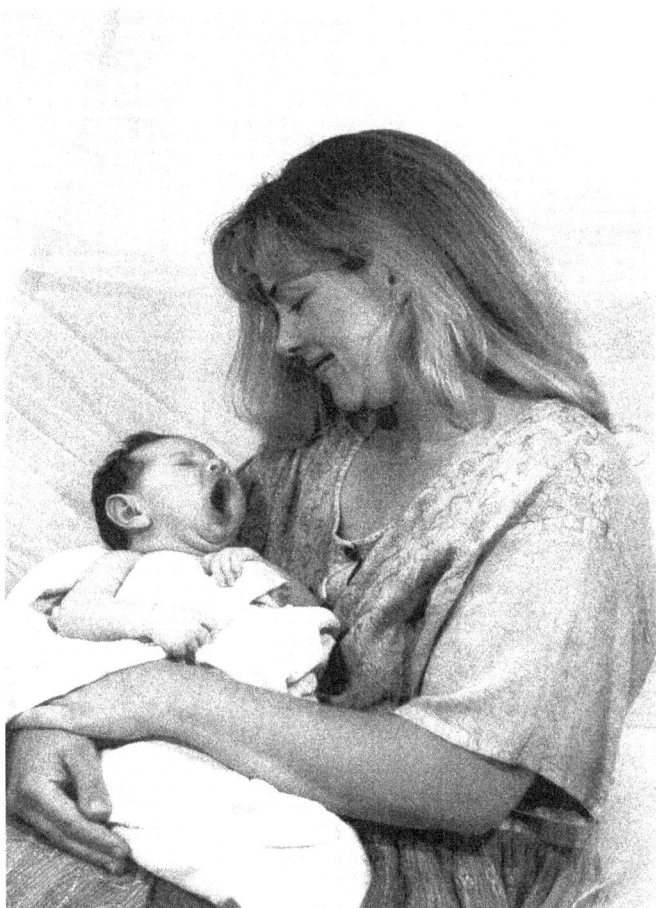

Nakiah & Mom

My husband and I were not feeling well at all.

I said, "Honey, do you love me?"

He said, "Yes, I love you."

I said, "Then will you take me out of my misery?"

He said, "No way! If I have to stay here, and suffer, so do you."

I said, "This is true love."

I Believe!

Ya know? I don't believe there really are bad people.

There are some who say we have people with no consciences, and that they were born this way, and this is how they will stay.

Some of us say there are bad people who have totally lost sight of that which is good. This idea implies that these people once knew right from wrong, but lost this knowledge along their way.

Was their goodness really lost? Were others really 'bad' from the start?

I must share what my 55 years have taught me. I believe that people get their goodness covered up by all the 'stuff'. Earth is incomplete - or maybe not…

But many of us get buried in resentment, anger, jealousy and other conditions familiar to limited human beings.

I was once told that we are all perfectly imperfect - which I have written in one of my books.

I was told that we are all marching together toward the infinite, and that we are all unique. I was told we all have a different story to tell.

The only way I can believe this is by knowing how my gifts were given to me. I feel that my goodness had to be uncovered, and the stuff cleared away, so that God could shine through me - causing my uniqueness and my gifts and blessings.

It seems that God might determine the uniqueness of every human being. To me there is no other way that so many humans can be different from each other.

I never believed snowflakes were all different until I got closer to God.

God is kind of powerful - having found a way to hang Earth out in the middle of space. If you cannot think of anything else about God, think about that.

I believe in God, equality, love, truth, grace, peace and just plain goodness.

Our country seems to believe in this also. For we are innocent until proven guilty, and we try to fit the punishment to the crime. Humans are more complicated than just innocent or guilty. If we cannot afford a lawyer, one is appointed to us at no cost.

We stand tall and reasonably free.

We, as a country, believe in life, liberty and the pursuit of happiness.

This goes for all people who are fortunate enough to believe.

And a small statement, with huge meaning, is stamped on our currency: IN GOD WE TRUST...

Have you heard this lately?

I pledge allegiance to the flag of the United States of America and to the republic for which it stands one nation under God, indivisible, with liberty and justice for all...

So, welcome to my world.
For I believe...

Messages

The Last few days the messages are very precise. They seem to either hit on the right or left side of my thighs - or else on my bottom.

When they happen on my bottom, it is as if I am receiving a disciplinary kick in the butt. They seem to say yes or no to what I think, hear or see.

These messages make me wonder how in the world people can know what I am thinking. They appear to read my mind!

I do a lot of guesswork - trying to figure out who or what may be causing this.

I have come up with many unusual scenarios. My main theory is still the same.

It is still the Super Humans giving me the guidance I never really had. They can be quite real at times, and this makes it very difficult for me to believe I have a mental illness.

Lots of times I go ahead and live my life just about as well as anyone. The other times I am driven to tears, pain, fear, and eventually I need hospitalization.

Most of the time I manage by using my list of 25 things I can do to feel better. I know most of them by heart, and I have printed them on the next few pages. They may work for you, as they have worked for me. I hope so anyway...

You may not have the same kind of struggles, but this list is pretty universal in its content and usefulness.

Sharing with you, gentle reader, has again given me support.

This journaling, of private thoughts, has turned into letters to you. I hope that you internalize some of the love and support in them.

My Tools for Living

(1) Lay under a blanket or sheet for a few minutes. (power rest)

(2) Do not isolate, yet at times, isolating is what helps...

(3) Change the subject by doing something you enjoy. Maybe do something for someone else.

(4) Call your therapist or someone else you trust. (Connecting is good medicine.)

(5) Talk to your significant other, or just be with him or her.

(6) Stay a healthy distance from people who are a vexation to your spirit.

(7) Take care of your mental health. (Realize that (angel) Dee doesn't want me to go "there". I'll feel bad…)

(8) Things always look better after 8 hours sleep.

(9) Realize you have a right to be heard, and a right to take up space.

(10) Leave the room or area if you feel uncomfortable. (Take a break.)

(11) Take a shower or bath.

(12) Listen to music or watch TV.

(13) Put on pajamas and slippers.

(14) Take back your power. (Do something to let you feel your personal power.) Something small may do it. (Turn on your radio...)

(15) Read this list.

(16) Hug someone or yourself.

(17) Drink extra water.

(18) Do deep breathing. (sitting or laying down)

(19) Have a cup of coffee or tea. (Take your time and enjoy.)

(20) Stretch (gently)

(21) Talk with God. (a higher power) Give thanks, and ask for peace.

(22) Realize that we are all perfectly imperfect. (limited human beings)

(23) Stay in control of any physical ailment you may have (to the best of your ability)…

(24) Let everyone have their "stuff", and don't take it personally.

(25) And last but definitely not least: Play, Have Fun, and Keep a Huge Sense of Humor!

There are more tools you could add to this list from your own life experience. They would be interesting to read!

I Am Going To Make It

I had an 'aha' today... I told my therapist that my sisters were telling me I should not be in the world-- That there was no place for me...

When I was young, I would back out of things. If I was with two or more people, I would withdraw as if I did not deserve to be there, or to be heard. I grew up just listening...

I may have begun to act as if everything was alright at two years of age. Everything was not alright...

gonna make it!

I found it necessary to either back out of our family gatherings, or to make people laugh. When I could make people laugh, I felt worthwhile. My place in the world was determined by my being able to keep the pain away from my mom and sisters.

I thought the pain was gone when I made levity happen, or when I stayed real quiet so I wouldn't burden people with my feelings.

For a long time I felt that my feelings could kill my Mom. I know she was quite 'down' to the extent that I always thought she was going to die.

She attempted suicide later on in my childhood, and much later was treated for Major Depression.

A lot happened to me at the age of two. I started being Mom's caretaker at two years old, when I began covering her up with a blanket. Later, I began to feel like her husband, and Jan became her confidante. I would fix cabinets and other things that maybe a husband would do. Jan would listen to all Moms' secrets about men friends, and other grownup subjects.

I can remember our plastic curtains and the chill of the rooms.

I once painted my whole bedroom with a two inch paintbrush--adding water to the paint, as there wasn't quite enough.

Jan was known as the 'bad' or 'rebellious' or the 'difficult' one. Mom would hit her quite a lot-- even at the dinner table. Mom may have broken Jan's spirit with all the whippings, and the weight of all those grownup problems...

Janice drowned the rest of her spirit in alcohol and cigarettes, and I feel she died of a broken heart at the age of 43. She was gone long before she passed away...

Since Jan and I were around each other a lot, I was whipped often too, but not as much as Jan. Mom and Jan had some sort of problem. Here too was desperation.

My spirit is very worn, because I don't remember being nurtured enough. I suffered from grave neglect and lack of guidance.

Mom even said I was so quiet she just thought I was fine and didn't need attention. Plus, I helped to make everyone a little happier. This made me seem really well adjusted.

So after talking with my therapist, I am entertaining the idea that my sisters just can't have me in *their lives*.

They are saying I have a
place in the world. They are not
telling me to die...

It occurred to me, just now, that
they cannot accept the adult Pat,
who is no longer just a joker and
a listener.

My value isn't measured,
anymore, as to how much I can
relieve my family's depression. I
am no longer an 'extra
wheel', or a 'just listening'
person.

I don't give anymore. I *share*.
This helps keep me from
becoming empty. I enjoy what I
call verbal tennis--where people
take turns talking and listening.

I am now standing tall, and am making a difference. For, at this late date, I have been given a gift that has already helped others, and has also made them chuckle at times.

Often, I don't know what is real and what is not, but not too long ago, I received a 'KEEP ON TRUCKING' award.

That is what I am now doing, with an added sense of purpose, and renewed will to live.

With good support from my psychiatric team, and love from 'my' dennis, I am going to make it!

KEEP ON TRUCKING!
FROM, A.C.M.H.C.

If It Ain't One Thing,
It's Another …

Have you ever noticed that, if you don't change, life comes along and kicks you in the butt until you do?

Someone else might say it differently, but it would mean the same thing.

This is one of the main reasons why people try so hard to be in control of something. Deep down we know that we can control very little.

I am told that we can only rule ourselves. This is nice in theory, but there is much we cannot rule - even in ourselves…

We can drink extra water, take
our meds and exercise.

We can breathe deeply, and
maybe recreate often.

We can structure our lives, and
get enough sleep, and we can
balance work with pleasure.

We can stay in the moment
instead of fretting about
yesterday.

Some of us build our muscles
and eat healthy. We learn
disciplines like Yoga, Aikido,
Karate and others.

The object may be self defense,
better health, confidence and a
larger respect for human life and
the rest of the universe.

We then feel that we have a "fighting chance" in an altercation, or a life threatening illness, or maybe we can avoid these things altogether.

We try to nurture our relationships, and contribute to our communities. We try to keep our heads above water--totally forgetting about the all familiar "factor" that is lurking just around the next corner.

'It' is hiding when you are all prepared for the day. You look and feel good. You have a full tank of gas. The sun is shining, and you have "everything under control". You think this is going to be a great day then ***it*** happens!

Your boss wants to see you in his office immediately! He has decided to give that promotion to someone else.

You slip on some ice, and hurt your toe. You limp around all day, while trying to avoid that person who got your job...

You see a gorgeous someone getting very chummy with your 'significant other'.

Then, you find that you forgot your billfold with your lunch money and driver's license. (You drove to work!)

You borrow some money for food. By now your carefully cultivated self esteem is faltering.

You're already not in control by early afternoon. If you're lucky, you find some way 'to turn things around'. If not, your day is ruined. That 'factor' has struck again, and you have lost that feeling of well being.

If we could flow along with each feeling that comes, if we could be pliant and bend instead of breaking, if we could be thankful for our lives - even when 'the sky is falling', we could stop in the middle of mayhem, and count our blessings. We could be thankful for what we still have, and we might not need to be in control so much.

Patricia A Fisher

I don't mean to push my belief
in God onto people, yet talking
to Him, while I am in turmoil,
builds a sort of bridge to get me
to a place of safety and
possibility.

I'm just so thankful to have
realized that the God I believe in
is not mean.

Sometimes he answers me
before I even finish my prayer...
This is very cool!

Dear God, Our Father,

Thank you for bringing us this
far. Thank you for the strength
of my country's people. Please
surround us with your
protection, and permeate us
with your love.

76

Stay close to all people, and let
them know how love feels. Let
them feel the wonder of equality,
and a strong sense of belonging.
Some have seldom felt
happiness. Please give them joy.

Let us each find a higher power
to give us hope, and to help us
honor each other.

With love from your creation,
In Jesus sweet name,

Amen

My therapist said,

"You know Pat; you
can ask him that
question."

Then I said,

"Hey, that's probably
A good way to get an
answer…"

AHA!

Can We Save the Planet?

I'm helping save the planet.
I just found a good way.

I'm being very prudent
'Bout what I do and say.

I didn't use to think I could
Do anything about it.

Thinking what just I could do,
Made me begin to doubt it.

This was very long ago.
At that age who could tell

What was realistic
Or what would ring a bell.

Tell me how to do this -
Not all by myself.

Let us help the people
Just like a Christmas elf!

So, I don't know
Just what to say.

This is a huge
Endeavor.

How can I
Explain to you?

Oh can I be
That clever?

First forgive
Who you have blamed.

Let them be
Just human.

Patricia A Fisher

Speak in such
A calming way,

Instead of always
Fumin!

The value of a human life
Could be recalculated.

The utter possibilities
Cannot, in words, be stated!

But we poets try and try
With all these combinations.

Those who work with numbers
Come up with long equations.

Those who operate on brains
With microscopic tools

Seem to want to know the truth,
And sometimes feel like fools.

Singers make angelic sounds -
Or sounds not so angelic,

To try and make us feel and be
As vital as a relic.

Painters capture what they want,
And leave the rest behind.

They try to make the world
Stand still with beauty that they
find...

Some know how to get along
From one day to the next.

This seems like a secret.
Is the answer found in text?

Actors are amazing,
When they do it right!

They are mesmerizing!
I watch them every night.

They keep us looking at the tube
An opiate of the masses,

Or there would be more criminals -
More people to harass us!

Have you noticed all the folks
Who live a life of service?

Many millions on this Earth
Both heal us and preserve us.

Actors, singers, people of God,
Doctors, nurses, "Yes", we nod.

What about construction workers -
Maybe even soda jerkers?

What about a banking teller?
What of an insurance seller?

We all might say firemen
Or cops we see. What of them?

I could go on,
But you can see,

How we help
Each other be.

If I dare to include you,
We could plan what we can do.

Each small difference
That we make

May just stop
A tummy ache,

Or maybe we can smile more -
Start out better than before.

Maybe we could recognize
A saddened look in someone's
eyes.

Say a prayer for him or her.
Compliments cost nothing per.

Give folks just one ray of hope.
For all of us need ways to cope.

Yes, we can all save this Earth.
Ask yourself just what it's worth.

One small action at a time,
As I write you in this rhyme,

Makes the world a happy place,
And puts that smile back on a
face.

Tomorrow I will go my way
With these words I wrote today.

A prayer of thanks I'll take
With me –
A prayer of our victory.

A little grin is on my face.
Dear God, I love the human race!

Remember when you
'found Your mouth',
And I told you that
You were all ass?

For a long time,
You were better.

But now, I think
You are coming out of
Remission...

A bit of funny
by
Patricia

Patricia A Fisher

Reach Out For Love

Bless my soul.
Sustain my life.

Make me smile
Through pain and strife.

I visit hell
Everyday.

I'll die if I
Keep on this way!

Similar blues
They sing in the south.

Open my ears,
And shut my mouth!

Hear with my soul,
And feel with my heart.

Cry all my tears,
And make a new start.

I pick myself up
By my bootstraps today.

"Impossibly done"!
The people all say.

But I know the secret
(Between you and me).

Just reach out for someone.
They might even be,

Pulling Those Boot
STRAPS
SUCCESSfULLY

Someone who's been there,
Though they didn't know

Something Impossible,
Moments ago,

Could be a success,
And easily done.

A little bit later
They love everyone.

Loving all people,
And reaching for one,

Then pulling those bootstraps,
When this is all done,

Maybe you thought
This all was a reach.

55 years
Isn't too old to teach!

I don't waste my time
By feeling real down,

By being just negative,
Hugging the ground.

For I get real busy,
And I move my butt!

For I just hate spending
My time in a rut!

I could have perished
Moments ago,

But then I reached out
Though I didn't know

This person I reached for
Was there before me

Feeling the pain
Then setting it free.

This person had heard,
"It cannot be done".

Then he reached out
For the love of someone...

REACH OUT FOR LOVE ♡

Is Too Much
Of A Good Thing

Really
Too Much?

Bitchy Woman

Today, I was real impatient!
I was very angry and frustrated
At people!

Later, I wanted to tip someone
For doing a great job
On my book.

Dennis told me we couldn't
Because of our budget.

I said that it was my Mom in me.
I reminded him that she was
Very generous,
And people thought
She was nice.

Then he said,
"No matter how much money
You give people,
You still won't be nice!"

A Heavenly Message

God Says:

Listen up little children!
This here's God!

Too many parents
Have spared the rod!

Latch key babies
On this Earth

Haven't had guidance
Since their birth!

Hate to tell you
What this can bring!

All these "babies"
Are floundering!

They don't even know
How to live,

How to make choices,
How to give.

This is the way
A person can be,

If all alone,
Since puberty.

Little guidance
No one home

To answer questions
Except by phone.

How alone
Would one child be,

If his parents
He could not see?

To ask his questions
He'd have to phone,

And he'd be forced
To stay alone.

It isn't the parent's
Fault, I guess.

But both have left
Their home a mess!

Chores and things
Do not get done.

Life gets hard
On everyone!

Pat Says:

"Are we making
More like me?

These kids may need
Therapy.

When I was young,
I'd make this vow,

I want my Mom home
With me now,

Even with
Less food to eat,

And holes in shoes
On both my feet.

There was much
We didn't own,

But worse than this
We were alone.

Now a broken
Family,

My two sisters
Cannot be

Within a mile
From my home.

They don't wish
To telephone...

They act like they're
Afraid to be

Part of a close
Family.

So that's just why
I say to you

Latch key babies
Quite a few

Have a difficult
Time these days,

Having problems
In many ways.

With no guidance,
As I've said,

Don't even know
The time for bed,

Or when to rise
And face the day.

Late for school,
This I say.

I was in
R.O.T.C.

It didn't last
Too long for me.

For I slept late,
And missed the drill.

Stayed up late,
I had no will,

To get up early
Everyday.

This is structure
People say...

Mom attempted
Suicide.

What would've happened
If she died?

Four little mouths
To be fed

We'd have starved,
If she were dead.

There, I've said
A bit 'bout mine.

Lots of times now
I feel fine!

Children without
Parenting

Have it rough.
To life they bring,

Hate, confusion,
Tears and rage.

It happens from
An early age.

I was brought up
With neglect.

Parents not there
To protect.

Latch key babies
I was one.

It really wasn't
Very fun!

Just a child
With no guide,

A latch key baby
How I cried...

No one home
To care for me,

So I grew up
Quite wild you see.

Discipline
Could not be found.

I ended up
Just running 'round.

With all the kids
Who drank and smoked.

Thank the Lord
That no one croaked!

But something died
Inside of me,

At that age
Just running free.

Punishment
Was here and there.

Whenever they
Had time to dare.

Patricia A Fisher

At these odd times
We got a beating.

Discipline
Was always fleeting.

I needed Mom
And Dad at home!

How painful
To be all alone!

To tell me what
Was right and wrong,

And let me know
That I belong.

To give support,
And help me share,

And let me know
How much they care.

It took me fifty
Years, and more,

To pick my pieces
Off the floor,

Internalizing
What was good.

I didn't know
How much I could

Love myself
The way I do--

Internalizing
Love of you.

Unconditonal
Love from fam'

Helps me know
Just who I am.

How can you measure

Who has it

Better or worse...

Where Do I Go From Here?

When I crash into hell
Here on Earth,
I want to die so badly,
But I never can end my life.

I spiral down so deep!
Yet, a spark is always there.
It keeps me wanting to survive...

It spills over onto 'my' Dennis,
When I am in hell.
How many times
Has he been hurt
By the force
That flows in and around me?

He never wants to separate
Or get a divorce...
He has made a commitment
He says...

He chooses to love me...
Where does love like that
Come from,
If not from God?

Dennis *is* love...
I must admit into evidence
That I am love too...
I always have had a
Huge capacity for love.

We met and stayed together,
Because we saw this
In each other.

I am standing tall again,
Since this writing.
It gives me strength,
And it brings me truth...

I learn from what I write.
Sometimes it makes me wiser,
And helps me read
My own mind...

God is with me at these times.
My being wiser comes from Him.
For He is also love
Just like Dennis and me
For we learned it from Him.
God is where I go from here.

One day, I was walking behind two men, who were chatting away.

While watching them, I suddenly realized that people really care about each other.

In The Name Of Love
(For Our Young-uns In Pueblo)

So happy I am,
Beginning once more
To share in the lives
Of those I adore.

I'm wanting to share
My love and my power.
With all of these 'young-uns',
At this very hour.

I give what I can
To strengthen the cause
Of all of our Family,
And Family-In-Laws.

I washed up her clothes,
And cooked her some meals.
With love in my heart,
I ask how she feels.

We three caught a bug.
We're coughing like mad!
Spitting and sputtering,
I am not sad...

'Cause we find our ways
To share a good word.
I'm asking myself,
"What was it I heard?"

My 'young-un' had tears
From a favor I'd done.
I told her, "It's love.
This makes it all fun!"

I'm not confused
At what is the truth.
Love is the answer.
I'm giving you proof.

Love is invisible.
And, when it stays,
It makes us all happy
On saddest of days.

Love in itself
Cannot be seen
Except on a face,
Calm and serene.

You can't see a heart
Beating with pride,
When love makes you feel
All funny inside.

Love is invisible-
'Cept on a face,
When we hold hands,
Or while we embrace.

Or when someone cares
With work that they do-
Honoring them,
And honoring you.

Respect and truth
Plus caring, I say,
Makes people happy
In a big way!

Again, love is seen,
In sparkling eyes,
In big cheery smiles,
Where nobody cries...

Though it's invisible,
Love gives us proof,
When someone cares,
With respect and with truth.

Dear 'little young-uns',
I want you to know,
That we have loved you
Since ages ago.

We think of you often.
We wonder if you,
Are doing ok.
To yourselves, be true...

Back then, you were tiny,
So full of life,
And now you have children
You've known joy and strife.

We are so proud
Of the old and the new.
You have come far.
May god bless you!

135

Patricia A Fisher

Dear Daddy,

You've been gone for almost 25 years...

Remember cherry peppers and shrimp dinners at Ciancios, buttermilk and soup at 3am after your work, and the boxes of fresh produce you brought us (from some kind of trading you managed to do)?

At 55, I am allowing these gifts into my life once more. For my pain is almost gone.

I remember now, how very proud you were, when you could say that we were your daughters. This may have been one of your most happy times in life.

3 AM With Daddy

Daddy, I have been so busy, feeling the pain of our difficult lives, that I almost missed what was good - until now.

Remember when I would climb onto the couch next to you, and play with your crew cut hair?

Remember when Janice and I would go with you to the VFW, and dance the jitterbug? We were quite the entertainers! Your friends would laugh and comment how grand we were. We were in hog-heaven!

As I look back, I see some good things that you brought into our lives.

Daddy, I am crying, and I miss you.

I would give a lot to be with you.

You made our house, and yard,
so beautiful! Landscaping is a
very difficult job to do. Yet, you
did all of ours, plus a lot more!

You use to trade junk with
acquaintances, and friends.
I remember when you carried a
surfboard down Larimer Street!
It was so oddly funny, because
we were smack in the middle of
Colorado, hence no big ocean
waves! Who knows where that
surfboard is today?

I'm smiling, now, while I see you
on your 'missions' in life. You
were always on the go... doing
something for someone...

Remember the tomato fight
between you and Mom? Mom got
mad at you for coming home
with rotten tomatoes. You two
started throwing them across
the dining room at each other!

God only knows what kind of
trade you made for those... Was
it for other junk? Was it for more
landscaping? Was it a trade for
whiskey? Who knows?

Even when you stopped
drinking, you would accompany
someone to a bar, or take a
bottle of liquor to a friend. I now
understand how that can be
done, as I am now on my 11th
year of abstinence... How do you
like that? I sense that this
makes you proud again.

I can recall some very good
advice from you, when I was 20
years of age. You said, "Instead
of so many pills, why not go dig
a hole, and cover it back up?"

When I was having a lot of
mental trouble, you said to, "Go
back to basics. Take a bath.
Brush your teeth. Comb your
hair."

Sometime, before I turned 9 or
10, you took the 4 of us-- plus
my little girlfriend-- to Mexico.
We had such a wonderful time!

We all fell in love with a beautiful
Mexican boy named Salvador.
(I would print his entire name,
but it has been 40 years, and I
cannot get his permission). Yet
his full name was like music...

He sold us huge hats and purses
that had chicken feathers on
them. The feathers were dyed
different colors. Mine were red!

Next thing I know, Dad, you
were wheelin'- n- dealin' again!
You had that same, pleased grin
on your face.

This little boy had a box of
Chiclets that he was trying to
sell. You offered him one price
for all his little boxes of gum.
The price was slightly lower than
if the boy sold them one by
one… But it was a good deal,
because this way he could sell
them all to you, make a profit,
and go home early.

The boy could not grasp this
concept, and said no.

To get to Mexico, we flew in Uncle Al's airplane. Remember? This was such a treat!

He had to take 3 of us, and then go back for the other 3.

I can remember his and Aunt Helen's home in Texas. It was so cold from their air conditioning, that, when I would open the door to go outside, the hot air was almost thick. You could cut it with a knife!

I'm sure you remember Woods Landing, Wyoming… We would go to this magical place, and we would ride horses, fish, light fireworks, and dance with each other in the gigantic dancehall!

To 'earn our keep', the children would sell fireworks, and serve food in the restaurant.

Country was the only music in the place, and cowboys, and their dates, would show up in western wear (of course)... The women were petite, and they wore these tiny little moccasins. It was kind of sweet how they would stand on their toes to hold onto their dance partner... (I wonder if the place is still the same...)

Daddy, Dennis and I are still married. I know how much you loved and respected him. He saw your virtues, and loved you also.

You know? I thank you and Mom for keeping Christmas in our lives. For I just know, down deep, that there was always Christmas... I love the season as you did. I can just see you grinning and giving again! I am like that, too. It is such a great excuse to give, and get, gifts! It is also an excuse to celebrate!

Now I have another excuse to celebrate! Our Nativity Scene has new meaning for me now...

I pray that you are being rewarded for all the effort you tried to put forth here on Earth. I, also, hope that you are at peace with Mom. You two lived a tortured life together, and you had love for each other. I just know it...

Also, try not to throw vegetables at each other! They are for eating! Ok?

Since this letter is to you, dear heart, I want to thank you for being my Dad...

At times, I just tell God, "Thank you for my life". Even when I am hurting, it is an amazing thing to just be alive!

So, I want you to know that I am fine, and I am thinking of you. Have fun up there, ok?

With love,
From your favorite Daughter!

Patsy

You can have action

Without happiness,

But you can't have

Happiness

Without action...

Lester W. Holley
(My Dad)

This is a note to my friend. She was with me through a childhood that could have been a lot worse without her...We have known each other clear from 6th grade, and, at that age, a kid needs a confidante to save him or her from the boogie man... or something worse...

After reading my autobiography, she called me on the carpet. She asked me why I kept so many things to myself over the years.

I thought about it a lot, then realized that maybe we *both* have a lot of catching up to do... I know very little about her during many of the years we were separated. Maybe she doesn't know that I missed her too...

As kids we didn't have a voice,
or a choice, but now we do.
I am looking forward to getting
reacquainted with my oldest and
'bestest' childhood friend…

Patricia A Fisher

Me and My Shadow

Silence was
my shadow
and 'twas
a prison too...

I have now
Grown out of it
And I sure have
Missed you!

We shared a world
Of make believe,
Though we went through
Hard times

And we both were
Punished,
As if
Commiting crimes!

As children,
We became quite close
I'm thankful
For this, too.

Life was just
Too difficult
Without a friend
Like you.

You've been my friend
'Bout 50 years.
I know
You're very kind.

This is why
I share with you,
And say
What's on my mind.

It was so good
To speak my piece,
When we were
On the phone.

And, all my life,
We've been the same,
Like we had both
Been cloned!

Yet, we were also
Different.
You'd been
Climbing trees!

As for me,
I'll share with you,
Some "jewels"
Such as these.

You're right,
I have been prissy.
It's all
I ever knew...

I don't climb trees.
I pick their fruit.
I'll make a pie
For you...

Maybe you are
Not like me.
We went our
Separate Ways.

And I would like
To speak to you
'Bout thoughts of
Yesterdays.

Do you feel
The same as me--
That, if you
Had a choice,

You'd have never
Gone away?
For children
Have no voice.

And we both needed
Much respect.
We needed
To feel valid.

We kept our secrets
To ourselves
Like voting
On a ballot.

So I went out
Into the world
Without my
Favorite friend.

My heart was
Truly broken.
I thought it
Wouldn't mend.

Silence was
My shadow.
Indeed, 'twas true
My dear.

But I have solved
The mystery,
And I am
Standing here,

Patricia A Fisher

Sad at how
I missed you,
Glad for
All we did,

And I have been
Too quiet,
Since I was
Just a kid...

My Buddy, My Cohort, My Friend

Our teacher in grade six
Perplexed and in a fix -

A student was now
Wearing on her nerves...

She made some strict
Announcements.

Then she
Raised her voice,

"Patsy's going to get
What she deserves!

You stay in for recess!
You're speaking way too loud!
Others have the manners
You do not!

Then you'll learn politeness,
And you will quiet down.

There's etiquette that you
Just haven't got!"

The teacher showed no
Manners.

She could have spoken low.

She didn't tell that girl
In privacy!

She was being testy -
Maybe even rude.

This is how the teacher
Seemed to me.

This child stayed inside,
While others went to play,

But something happened,
As a big surprise!

Someone else was in the room.
She seemed to be real prissy,

But wasn't wearing clothes
A rich girl buys...

This prissy girl was quiet,
And her eyes were full of tears.

She felt as if she couldn't
Even speak.

But she told this student,
"You must know I am shy.

I feel, today
Is looking rather bleak."

Patricia A Fisher

Then she shared a fun thing,
"My name is Patsy, too!

There's one thing now
In common that we have...

Both our names are Patsy.
Now isn't that a hoot?

This gives us one more reason
For a laugh!"

This was all we needed.
We giggled all through lunch.

We liked each other
Very much indeed!

For we were both quite different.
She was not like me.

A real tom boy she was
We both agreed...

162

We both stayed in for recess.
The reason became clear,

As she asked me
Why I even stayed.

I thought the teacher
Spoke to me,

When she called out
Your name,

But now, I guess, it seems
We both have paid."

This was our great beginning.
Our friendship was quite grand!

Together, as we were,
Most everyday.

For Mom divorced my Daddy,
And I was still in shock.

Still quiet,
I heard Patsy talk away!

She and I grew up
Together everyday.

My sense of humor
Grew, and grew, and grew.

For if I didn't laugh a lot,
I'd cry and feel real bad.

At these times, I'd not know
What to do...

Patricia A Fisher

Pat and I
Found happiness

In spite of
Everything.

She and I found
Laughter

In whatever
Life would bring.

Some forty-five
More years it's been.

Patsy married
Kenny.

All the good times
We have had -

You might say there
Were plenty!

They had a
Son and Daughter.

Grandchildren,
They had four.

They have such
Abundance!

Who could ask
For more?

Patsy had
So much to say.

We'd laugh
When times were bad.

She has been a good,
Good friend.

One of the best
I've had.

She stood up
By my side.

She was my
Maid of Honor.

She stood there
By my side,

Or I'd have been
A gonner!

If I was getting
Married,

Alone with my
True love,

Stress sure would've
Killed me.

For weddings
From above,

Patricia A Fisher

Still can make you nervous -
Though this is your big day.

A friend can come in handy,
If you faint dead away!

170

Patricia A Fisher

The Wedding
November 17, 1973
(By My Dad)
Lester Warren Holley

This is the day
God set apart
Just for you both
To get a new start.

There is an answer
To all you may ask.
It isn't going to be
Much of a task

You must be honest
In all that you do.
Love each other.
Unto yourselves be true.

172

From This Day Forward

Things like this
Are not for men to judge.
Make sure your friendship
Will never budge

Denny you need a friend
Even more than a wife.
Patsy you need a friend
Even more than your life.

God has funny ways
In matters like this.
He never makes it
All rainbows and bliss.

Love is something
That makes everyone feel,
But you must stay friends
To make it real.

173

I stand here
With a tear in my eye.
Denny you surely are
A lucky guy.

Patsy on you your
Family must center.
Never leave room
For the devil to enter.

This is the epistle
Just for the today.
I love you both
In a special way.

Daddy

The Author 1973

175

My Mama and Me

Daddy Giving Me Away

Mr. and Mrs. D. H. Fisher

*Patsy Stevens and Me
Goofing Around!*

Author Pummeled With Rice
(When It Was Still Allowed)

From This Day Forward

To you,
 I dedicate my life.
The last thirty years
I've been your wife

You can place your dreams
Upon my heart,
As we begin
A brand new start.

Thirty more years
Again with you,
As we begin
Our lives anew ,

Each day, to you
I'll make this vow
I'll love you forever
Here and now.

Dear Patricia,

This is your best book so far! I've loved you for thirty years. And here is to thirty more!

Love, Dennis

www.ingramcontent.com/pod-product-compliance
Lightning Source LLC
Chambersburg PA
CBHW072227270326
41930CB00010B/2021